To
  Zachary
    Cameron
      & Richie

Just a peek into our
World! your Mom's & Mine!

:)

Love ya,
Auntie Lissa

When Mother Was
Eleven-Foot-Four

When Mother Was Eleven-Foot-Four

A Christmas Memory

Jerry Camery-Hoggatt

Fleming H. Revell
A Division of Baker Book House Co
Grand Rapids, Michigan 49516

Published by Fleming H. Revell
a division of Baker Book House Company
P.O. Box 6287, Grand Rapids, MI 49516-6287

Second printing, August 2002

Printed in the United States of America

Library of Congress Cataloging-in-Publication Data

Camery-Hoggatt, Jerry.
     When mother was eleven-foot-four : a Christmas memory / Jerry Camery-Hoggatt.
        p.   cm.
     ISBN 0-8007-1789-9
     1. Christmas—Miscellanea. 2. Camery-Hoggatt, Jerry—Child-hood and youth. I. Title.
BV45 .C284 2001
277.3'0825'092—dc21
[B]   2001019700

For current information about all releases from Baker Book House, visit our web site:

http://www.bakerbooks.com

For Bill and Lauren Younger
Givers of Extravagant Gifts
Agents of Grace

one

This is the story of the Christmas of 1963, which is the Christmas that I learned what it means to be a giver of gifts. But this story isn't about me. This story's about my mother.

My mother's name was Josephine Mary Knowles Hoggatt, but everybody called her simply "The Lady," because in our town she was a woman of stature.

My mother was eleven-foot-four.

Okay, she wasn't eleven-foot-four *all* the time, just *some* of the time. She was eleven-foot-four when she needed to be. Most of the time she was four-foot-eleven. She was a tiny little woman––on the heaviest day of her life she weighed less than a hundred pounds—but she always said that when she was at her very best, she was eleven-foot-four.

Whenever she would say, "I drew myself up to my full height, and . . ." we knew we were about to hear a story of some encounter in which she had demonstrated that even a person who was tiny on the outside could be large on the inside.

You should have seen my mother when she was eleven-foot-four.

This really happened: When Mother was in her sixties she ran a home for delinquent boys—"The Tujunga Ranch Home for Boys," she called it. It was my tiny white-haired mother and fourteen juvenile delinquents.

One of the boys in the Tujunga Ranch Home was a tough little guy named C.J., whose older brother was a member of the Hell's Angels motorcycle gang. One Saturday morning my mother was awakened by the sound of banging on her front door and the revving of motorcycle engines in the driveway. When she went to the door to see who it was, there stood C.J.'s older brother, pounding on the door with the butt end of a bowie knife. To hear the boys tell the story later, C.J.'s brother was seven feet tall, tattooed everywhere, and wearing a way-too-small black T-shirt with a skull printed on the back.

He scowled at my mother. "Lady," he growled. "I'm giving you just ten minutes to get C.J. and all his stuff out here on the porch."

My mother looked C.J.'s brother straight in the eye and said, "Young man, I'm giving *you* just two minutes to get off my property." Then she drew herself up to her full height, looked *down* at him, and held her gaze steady.

He blinked first.

"Yes, ma'am," he said. With that, he turned around, climbed back on his motorcycle, and drove away. He took his gang with him, and Mother never saw him again.

After that, she never had any trouble with her fourteen juvenile delinquents, either, but it wasn't because they had seen her stare down a member of the Hell's Angels motorcycle gang. Her boys didn't give her any

trouble because they had all seen for them-
selves what my mother was like when she
was eleven-foot-four.

My mother could be as tough as nails when
she needed to be.

My father's name was William Hoggatt, but
everybody called him by his middle name,
Kelly. He was a tall, angular, good-looking
man who didn't know he was good-looking.
He wore a wide-brimmed gray felt hat pulled
low over one eye, which gave him rather a
rakish look. Sometimes he wore the collar of
his shirt outside the collar of his sport coat.

It was a look that eventually went the way of the big bands, but in the fifties it was high style, "genuine Saville Row," my mother said. More than once I saw my father turn the heads of married women when we made our way to our table at Bob's Big Boy restaurant after church.

I didn't know my father was good-looking either, but I can tell you when I found out. Mount Craig Summer Camp, 1961. I was eleven years old. My father was unloading our stuff from the back of the station wagon while we carried everything up to the cabin. From the door of the cabin I looked back, ostensibly to see how he was doing, but really to check out the girls. To my absolute astonishment, the girls were checking out my dad.

"Who was that man?" one of the girls asked as she watched my father drive away. I found out later her name was Leslie.

"That's my father," I said.

"You gonna grow up to look like him?" Leslie asked.

"That all depends. What do you think of my father?"

"I think your father is a very good-looking man," she said. There, it was out in the open.

"Well, then, in that case, I will," I said.

It didn't happen. I ended up favoring my mother, but Leslie never knew that. Before the week was over she had become the first girl I ever kissed. I suppose in my more honest moments I realize that I owe my father a debt of gratitude for that kiss, but I never told him. I don't think he would have approved. After all, I was only eleven.

William Kelly Hoggatt was a man of principle. His principles were always strange to me—sometimes they obligated him to do things that my principles now prohibit—but right now I want to honor the fact that he was measuring his life against a yardstick larger than his own vested interests. He charted his course by a compass outside himself, and he was absolutely committed to following whatever path that course required, never mind the consequences. Consequences were absolutely beside the point, he said.

If you had asked my father to list the virtues of a principled man, he would have told you that pride of place at the top would go to honesty and that running a close second place would be consistency. Now, that's a little odd, really. People don't usually think of consistency as a virtue, but it was for my father. For him, consistency was a theological virtue because *God* was consistent—"the same yesterday, today, and forever," he often said, "and anybody who wants to be like God should be consistent, too."

The upside of my father's consistency was that he was absolutely reliable. If he said he would be somewhere, he would be there. If he said he would do something, he would do it. If he said he would cover some expense, you could trust that it would happen. He was dyed-in-the-wool, take-it-to-the-bank reliable, my father was.

There were two downsides to my father's insistence on living his life consistently. The first was that he was predictable. He didn't approve of surprises. He ran his whole life by the budget, the calendar, and the "to do" list.

The second downside to my father's consistency was that he was inflexible. He didn't approve of compromise any more than he approved of surprises. Compromise meant not only that you were weak, it also meant that you had no scruples, no character. When I was ten years old, my father and I had an argument about some matter or another. As I recall, it had something to do with whether or not I could go horseback riding with some friends. I laid out my case. When I was finished, my father looked at me and said that I was right, my evidence was good, and my reasoning was logical, but his mind had already been made up, and he was going to stick with his original decision.

"If I change my mind now," he said, "you'll think you can change my mind about other things, and there'll be no end to the negotiating. I don't intend to spend my life bandying words with a ten-year-old!"

If my mother could be as tough as nails, my father could be as hard as flint. He was the best and the worst of what it meant to be a realist. He was a realist, he said, because God is a realist.

But Mother was a romantic. Ask Mother for a list of virtues, and right at the top would be honesty; that much she shared with my father, but for her, right next to honesty came not *consistency* but *wisdom*.

My mother agreed with my father that there was an important place for the budget, the "to do" list, and the calendar. It's important to carry your own weight, to pay your own way. "Keep your promises," she told us. "Be where you say you'll be. Live within your budget. Keep a stiff upper lip. Stay the course. Endure. Live within limits." One ought to do such things as a matter of course, she always said.

Except sometimes.

Sometimes, my mother said, you have to set the calendar aside and hit the road with no destination, no map, and no deadline, and just see where the road takes you. "We'll just follow our nose," she said.

Sometimes you have to set aside the "to do" list and spend the day soaking up the afternoon sun. Or kick off your shoes and dangle your feet in a stream. Once she checked us out of school early to go fishing, not because she didn't respect school but because she wanted us to know firsthand that being industrious was only one part of living a good and full life.

She felt that way about the budget, too. "Sometimes you have to set aside the budget and do something absolutely extravagant," she said, "something your head tells you you can't afford and your heart tells you you can't do without."

Mother said that the ability to know when it was right to do such things was *wisdom*, and more than once she told us that the inner personal freedom to do something absolutely extravagant is the closest human beings ever come to understanding what God must feel when he is being gracious. This was especially so in the giving of gifts. According to Mother, when we give someone else an extravagant gift, we somehow rise above ourselves, even if only just a little bit. We become better than we are, she said, larger on the inside.

My mother said she was a romantic because God was a romantic. She even had a romantic picture of what God looked like, to match his romantic character. The God in my mother's imagination had dark, wavy hair, longish and tossed back, with flecks of gray at the temples, and a carefully trimmed black mustache. He had shockingly clear eyes. Mother said whenever she imagined God, he was wearing a black tuxedo with a red cummerbund, and a white silk scarf over his neck for style. Mother said that in her mind's eye God looked for all the world like Omar Sharif. (For my younger readers, my mother's God looked like Yanni with a haircut.)

Mother was a romantic because she believed in her heart of hearts that God was a romantic and that anybody who wanted to be like God should be a romantic, too. That's the way she lived her life. When she turned sixty-three she sold The Tujunga Ranch Home for Boys and hit the road for the big adventure that had always filled her dreams. For more than a year we got postcards from Mother from all over the world—from Europe, from the Holy Land, from Turkey. Once she wrote that she was living in a cardboard box in Mexico.

Before my mother died she told us that she didn't want a funeral. "Invite everyone over and have a barbecue," she said.

She didn't want a hearse, either. "Hire a Dixieland band and dance my coffin to the cemetery," she said. In the end, we did have the barbecue, but we had a memorial service, too, out of consideration for Mother's many friends. The only thing that prevented the Dixieland band was that she had decided at the last minute to have her remains cremated and thrown to the wind—a fitting symbol for the free spirit at the core of who my mother was.

Now, when you get two people as different as my mother and father, and as committed as they were to honesty—which they both took as the highest virtue—sparks fly. My mother and my father were champion arguers. They fought about everything. They fought about what we should wear to school. They fought about what color we should paint the house. They fought about whether or not we should admit Red China to the United Nations. They fought about whether or not there should *be* a United Nations.

But there was absolutely nothing my parents fought about with greater passion or more intensity than the whole matter of Christmas gift giving. They didn't fight about what presents we should or shouldn't get—they fought about whether or not we should get any presents at all.

My father was opposed to Christmas gift giving on principle.

two

We lived in a great big, old, lumbering three-story gray clapboard house that had at one time been a church. You could still see traces of the church in the structure of the building, like the paired windows on either side of the first floor where the sanctuary had been. The paired windows were set up to correspond with the ends of the pews. The first floor had high ceilings and double doors that opened onto what had at one time been the church narthex.

The family actually did its living on the second floor where the parsonage had once been. There was a living room, a kitchen, my parents' room, a room for the girls, and a bathroom with a tub where we held family conferences. The third floor had been the church's attic, which my father finished off as a dormitory for the boys.

Eight children lived in the house—myself, my sister, our three brothers, and our three cousins—Joyce, John, Jim, Jerry, Joel, Small Nathan, Vickie, and Pudge. Two girls. Six boys. Our cousins lived with us because our uncle Big Nathan was a single father, and he was in the navy and was stationed overseas for months at a time.

Between the second and third floor of the house my father had built a steep staircase, closed off on the bottom by a door. He intended the door as a way of closing off noises from the dormitory in the evenings when he and my mother entertained guests, but for us it served another purpose. The door meant we could slip down into the stairwell late at night in our pajamas and listen to our parents fight.

The fighting about Christmas presents always began sometime in early November. They had their moments, my mother and father, but these were the most colorful. Mother and Father—an extravagant giver of gifts and a man of principle, one as tough as nails, the other hard as flint, both committed to honesty as the first virtue, both determined to do what was right, neither one willing to compromise. The fights about Christmas presents were always terrifying and wonderful to hear.

Let me pause here and say that my father was not tightfisted in any sense. He was careful with his money, but within what he could afford he was a generous man. He made up for missing Christmas with a lavish pile of birthday presents, but he was opposed to Christmas itself. He and my mother went at it every year, and it was always the same. The only things that changed from year to year were the intensity, the volume, and the determination they each showed not to lose this particular battle. The fights always ended with the same result, too, but it was never something we could take for granted, and so year after year we found ourselves in the stairwell, listening to our parents fight about Christmas.

We six boys would slip out of bed and sneak down the stairs and listen, afraid to breathe, knowing that however the argument turned out would determine how Christmas would be this year. Every November it went like this:

Mother started off: "Come on, Kelly. Sooner or later we're going to have to talk about the Christmas presents."

"Not this again," said my father. "You already know how I feel about all that."

"Maybe not. Maybe you've changed your mind somehow."

"Well, I haven't," said my father. (How could he change his mind? That would be inconsistent.) "Okay, I'll say it: I don't think we should give the children Christmas presents this year."

"Why not *this* time?" asked my mother.

"Christmas is too commercialized," said my father. "It's been taken over completely by the pagans. You know how I feel about that."

By "pagans" my father meant everyone who would make a buck on Christmas, and that included the atheists who sold things to Christians at a profit. And Jews. And Catholics. And Episcopalians, who were after all almost Catholic. And Lutherans. And

Methodists. And Baptists. Mostly anyone who wasn't a Pentecostal.

My mother agreed with my father that Christmas had been taken over by the pagans, but in her view we should take it back. Besides, she said, she didn't have any problem with someone making a buck on Christmas, so long as the buck was earned honestly and legally. "After all," she reasoned, "the people who make that buck will work hard for it. A lot of them will work overtime. They'll probably use it to pay the rent, or put food on the table, or buy Christmas presents for their own kids."

"It's bad business, mixing up Christmas with money," he said. "People get all the wrong ideas about gifts and gift giving from doing that." My father said that what really stuck in his craw was the idea that you could somehow *earn* the gifts.

"Now, where would you get a cockamamie idea like that? And what on earth does any of that have to do with Christmas?" Mother wanted to know.

"You know exactly what it has to do with Christmas, Jo," said my father. "Santa Claus is out there, keeping a list of who's naughty and who's nice. Giving gifts only to nice kids but cutting out the naughty ones. It messes up their understanding of what gift giving is all about. Turns the whole thing into a business transaction. Give a gift that way, and it's not a gift at all. It's payment for services rendered."

"Oh, for heaven's sake, Kelly, they're children." Mother's voice showed her exasperation. "They aren't going to go down that path. Only somebody who thinks like you would come up with reasoning like that. They don't think like you. Trust me on this one." Mother was growing impatient.

My father was growing impatient, too. He said the bottom line was that he didn't want *his* kids growing up with the mistaken idea there was anything at all about gifts and gift giving and Christmas that could be turned into a business transaction, giving in order to get, being good in order to get more presents, payment for services rendered.

Mother said she didn't want *her* kids growing up with the mistaken idea that if you wanted to find joy in your religion you had to convert and join the pagans.

When my father heard that, he knew he was in over his head so he just flat-out pulled rank instead. "You don't understand, Jo," he said. "It's *my* decision. *I'm* the head of this house. *I* bring home the bacon, *I* write the bills, *I* put the bread on the table, and *I* decide whether or not there will be Christmas presents this year. As head of this house, I withhold permission." This final phrase—I withhold permission—was delivered slowly, ponderously, with an air of finality about it: "I . . . withhold . . . permission."

Behind the door, we six boys caught our breath. Even though I was too young to understand my father's argument, I knew from his tone that he was laying down the law. When Father laid down the law, it was nothing to be trifled with. How was Mother going to get past that? Everything depended on what she said next. In the silence we could feel more than hear, as our mother drew herself up to her full height. When she spoke, her tone had its own air of finality about it.

"No, Kelly," she said. "*You* don't understand. I'm not asking for permission. I'm inviting you to join me in signing the cards."

Behind the door, six young boys scurried up the stairs and back to bed. There would be Christmas. There would be presents. There was a God. God looked like Omar Sharif.

three

In the end, my father compromised with my mother, as he did every year. He always ended up compromising with my mother in three specific ways.

The first was that he allowed her to get a Christmas tree. He even put money in the budget for a six-foot tree. What he couldn't prevent was her habit of adding to the Christmas tree budget—what she called scrinching and sockofissing. She saved out nickels and dimes from the change at the Piggly Wiggly Market when she went grocery shopping. She horse-traded green stamps. I remember her doing the neighbor's ironing—sprinkling the shirts with a mixture of starch and water from a Coca-Cola bottle, then rolling them tight and storing them in the refrigerator until she could get to them late at night, after she had finished her own chores and put her children to bed.

Sooner or later, inevitably, she added enough money to my father's tree budget to buy a twelve-foot Christmas tree.

My mother bought her Christmas tree every year on the first Monday of December. She would do this on a weekday because my father was at work, and she knew it was hard for him. She always bought her tree from Ollie Flory, who ran the roadside peanut stand a mile up the highway. Every year Mr. Flory supplemented his income by setting up a Christmas tree lot next to his peanut stand. He always hauled the tree home for us in his truck, partly as a courtesy and partly because he took a special delight in helping my mother turn this part of my father's Christmas philosophy on its head. Mr. Flory didn't much like my father. He always gave my mother a poinsettia plant to go with the tree, as a bonus for the big sale, Mother said, but we knew it was because my father would disapprove. Mother placed the poinsettia on the stairs with a sigh, I think because it reminded her that there were other romantics in the world. According to my father's definition, Mr. Flory wasn't a romantic. He was one of the pagans.

They started early because they had to "do the deed," Mr. Flory said, before my father got home. Mr. Flory would cut off an inch or so from the trunk of the tree and then some of the lower branches, too, so my mother could scatter pine branches around the house and arrange candles among them. My mother said she loved the smell of pine needles in the house at Christmastime.

Then Mr. Flory and my mother and anyone else who was around would swing open the wide double doors and muscle the tree past what had been the narthex and into the sanctuary. They had to set it up on the first floor because that was the only place in the house that had high enough ceilings. It was the only Christmas tree I ever saw inside a house that had to be held in place with guy wires.

Then Mother decorated, standing on a chair and starting with the popcorn strings. The thing about popcorn strings is that you have to pop the popcorn weeks early and set it out so it can go stale. My mother had strings of other things, too—silver balls, and paper chains, and cutout dolls—but she liked the popcorn strings best, she said, because they reminded her of the war years when everybody had to make do or do without. She said they reminded her of the Christmases she spent praying for her brothers on the front or on ships all around the world, and how grateful she was that they'd all come home safe from the war.

Sometimes she added cranberries in among the popcorn to give a kind of red-white motif. She also added strings and strings of lights. She had strings of those big-bulbed colored lights that gave off a soft glow among the branches, and then in among these she added strings of tiny pinpoint white lights. Over the whole thing she scattered bits of that silvery tinsel that's supposed to look like icicles. She was always careful to scatter the tinsel where it would reflect the light from the strings of bulbs.

Then she got out her collection of ornaments. Some of her ornaments were ready-made. She and her brothers and her sister exchanged store-bought ornaments every year, and she traded ornaments with childhood friends and friends from the church, and over the years her collection had grown very large. In fine indelible ink on each one she wrote the date and the name of the person who had given it to her, and as she took them one by one out of their boxes she commented on the donors—how they met, why they were important, how long it had been since they had seen each other, what they had done that year, what hopes she had for them this year. Sometimes she just sighed. She was like an archeologist, unearthing treasures from their crypts in the boxes she kept in the large space beneath the stairwell. We learned our family history again every Christmas as Mother decorated her twelve-foot Christmas tree.

Among my mother's store-bought decorations were four little dancing girls, each with an opening to hold a tiny candle, and each with one of the letters of the word N • O • E • L. (When Mother wasn't looking, my brother John always rearranged the letters to spell L • E • O • N instead.)

Far and away my mother's favorite ornaments were the little handmade ones we brought home from Sunday school every year. She had hundreds of these tiny little ornaments made by unskilled stubby children's fingers. There were pictures of her children pasted on cardboard backing and ringed about with glued-on Cheerios. There were little plastic baby Jesus figures glued into walnut half-shells—"the gospel in a nutshell," my Sunday school teacher had called them. There were "angels" made out of white paper plates with the wings cut out of the curve of the plates and the faces of her children pasted in where the faces of the angels should have been. There were handprints pressed into clay tablets, brought home from school, and when Mother hung them on the tree they weighed the branches down so low they brushed the floor. She had a whole collection of tiny stuffed toys, sent by a friend when my parents were newly married and had nothing besides popcorn strings for their first tree. She kept all these handmade Christmas decorations from year to year, too, and the collection of personal memories that were attached to them was a source of wonder to me.

If the glory of our house was my mother's twelve-foot Christmas tree, the crowning glory of the Christmas tree was her guardian angel. It was a twelve-inch doll she had inherited from her own mother. It had a finely detailed porcelain head and wings spread wide and a gossamer gown of antique lace.

My family followed the custom of allowing the youngest child in the house to place the angel on the tree as the final ornament, the *coup de grace*. This presented a rather unique problem at our house. The youngest child in our family was my cousin Pudge. A twelve-foot tree has a deep circumference, and even when Pudge stood on a ladder he couldn't reach high enough or deep enough to put the angel on the top branch.

My brother John solved this problem with a brass ring, a paper clip, and a fishing pole. He sewed the brass ring to the angel's dress right between the places where its wings connected to its shoulder blades. He made a hook from the paper clip and tied the hook to the fishing line. Then he simply lowered the angel into place like a crane operator. When the hook slipped out of the brass ring, Pudge threw the wall switch that turned on the lights, and then, all at once, magically, it was Christmas.

The neighbors would come for the evening, and we'd all drink wassail and cider and sing Christmas carols. They would already be there when my father got home from work, so how could he object? I think he was always dazed a little by the change Mother's Christmas tree made in the atmosphere of the house. Even a realist has to admit the presence of magic like that when he sees it. My mother's Christmas tree was a sight to behold.

The second way my father compromised with my mother was that he allowed her to give us things we would have gotten anyway, which basically meant underwear and socks and T-shirts. We hated getting underwear and socks and T-shirts for Christmas. It seemed like such a cheat.

For us kids, the worst part about getting underwear and socks and T-shirts came later, on the first day back to school in January when our mother made us wear our new clothes. Somehow we had it in our heads that only the poor kids got underwear and socks and T-shirts for Christmas, and that by wearing new clothes the first day back to school we were signaling the world that we were poor. We begged our mother to let us wear old clothes, like the rich kids.

She never did that, but I think she understood our dilemma. Once when I was grown I asked her about that, and she said she included underwear and socks and T-shirts because that was the only way she could include my father's name on the cards as a giver of Christmas gifts. I think she hoped that we would think more kindly of my father and his convictions about Christmas gift giving. In an odd way, that was her gift to him.

The third way my father compromised with my mother had to do with something Mother called "The Snake Room."

I said that we lived in a three-story house, but that isn't quite the truth. Our house backed up against a hill, and the builder had built an entry directly out from the second floor onto the roadway that ran behind. That meant that the house had three stories on one side and two on the other. The builder hadn't excavated the slope of the hill but had left the slope as a kind of slanted crawl space at one end. Where the slope of the hill intersected with the ground of the first floor he had built a wall, behind the platform where the pulpit had stood. In the wall was a small door.

My mother called the room behind the door "The Snake Room."

"Why?" I asked once, when I was maybe eight.

"Because that's where the snakes are," Mother said. "And spiders, too. Huge spiders, some of them as big as your father's hand.

Tarantulas. Nasty things. Don't you ever go in the Snake Room."

"But what do the spiders and snakes eat in there?" I asked. "Do you feed them?"

"No," she said. "They eat each other. Awful mess. They eat little boys, too."

"But we're all here, alive," I said. "Count us. We're all here. They haven't eaten any of *us*."

"They haven't eaten any that you know about, child," Mother said. "What if there were others who came before you? Never ever go in the Snake Room."

I dropped the subject after that because it made my flesh crawl. I just didn't know for sure.

But I didn't stop thinking about it. One day, I think late in October, it got to be too much. I did what I had to do. After all, I was eight years old.

I went in the Snake Room.

It ruined Christmas for me that year.

The Snake Room was where my mother hid her Christmas presents. She had hundreds of presents in there. Boxes of them. Bags of them. Secreted away. Not organized so much as stashed. She bought Christmas presents all year long. After-Christmas sales. Year-end clearance sales. No sales at all.

My mother was a keen observer of her children's eyes, and whenever any little thing lit a spark in a child's eyes, Mother would go back later and add that something to her booty. She stashed it all in the Snake Room.

There's no lonelier feeling than the feeling that comes over you when you realize that, of all eight kids in the house, you're the only one who knows what the real Christmas presents are going to be and you can't say a word to anybody. Then it dawns on you that on Christmas morning you're going to have to fake it. There's no lonelier moment than that.

So I went and got my little brother Joelie. Showed him. It took the edge off my guilt, and I knew that if I got in trouble I wouldn't be in trouble alone.

My father's compromise with the Snake Room came on Christmas Eve, after we kids had all gone to bed. Even though he disapproved of my mother's extravagant Christmas gift giving, he stayed up all night on Christmas Eve helping her wrap presents. They'd usually finish just as the sun was coming up, which meant that they were dropping into bed exhausted just as we were waking up. We would have to wait until later in the day for my parents to wake up before we could actually open anything, but they always let us at least sort our presents into piles while we waited. We rattled them and hefted them and pressed their sides. We sorted them and then sorted them again. We *prioritized* them. But we had to wait for our parents to get up before we could actually open them.

Mother would get up, fix herself a cup of coffee, and join us in the sanctuary. Then pandemonium would break loose.

Even now I can see my mother standing there in her bathrobe in the doorway, coffee cup in hand, watching us as we tore into the packages. She surveyed the room like this every year, drinking in the sights and sounds and smells of Christmas.

There was the twelve-foot Christmas tree, decorated with the ornaments of people she loved, all with stories to tell—the history of her family and friends. On the tree, the lights and the popcorn strings to remind us of the war years when everybody had to make do or do without, and her joy that her brothers had come home safe from the war.

There was the poinsettia on the stairs that Mr. Flory had given her to remind her that there were other romantics in the world.

There were the children, all eight of us, still in our pajamas but no longer sleepy—myself and my sister and our brothers and our cousins, wearing cowboy boots with our pajamas, with holsters and silver cap guns and cowboy hats with the lanyard trim threaded into holes that had been punched along the rim. We rode stick horses with upholstered plastic heads. We lassoed the dogs and shot off our cap guns and generally made it impossible for our parents to go back to sleep.

There were the piles of shredded wrapping paper, paper she tried every year to salvage and save for the year following, but always in vain.

There were the two dogs—Sancho, our collie pup, and Ferdinand, the little bull terrier—

romping and playing with the wrapping like it was a kind of canine catnip.

In the background were the sounds of my mother's old record player, with Bing Crosby dreaming of a white Christmas or Gene Autry singing about Rudolf the Red-Nosed Reindeer.

And of course, through it all, there was the subtle pervasive smell of the pine needles.

Once I paused long enough to gaze at my mother as she drank in this reverie, and suddenly I realized that I was seeing her in a new light. This was what my mother was like when she was at her very best. As tiny as she was, standing there in the doorway, in my heart, too, my mother was eleven-foot-four.

It was a flash, a momentary vision, gone as quickly as it had come, but it left an impression so strong that even now when I close my eyes it still comes back. She was eleven-foot-four, because, in spite of all obstacles, and in the teeth of my father's objections, she had made this all possible.

four

Something happened to my family during the summer of 1962, something that shouldn't be part of a Christmas story, so I'm not going to tell you what it was.

But I will tell you this: It was decisive, it happened all at once, and it was irreversible. So far as my mother's world was concerned, it was catastrophic. In the space of half an hour after this event my father was gone from our home forever.

Within a month my older brother John was out of the house, living in his truck. My sister was already grown and gone. My uncle

Big Nathan had already left the navy, married my aunt Nadine, and had taken our cousins—Small Nathan, Vickie, and Pudge—back to live with them.

My mother was suddenly on her own, a single mother trying to raise her three youngest sons—Jim, myself, and Joelie. She had no education to speak of, had not finished grammar school because of the Depression and after that, the war. She had never worked outside of the home, and she had no marketable job skills.

Within two months the house was gone.

My mother and we boys moved into a kind of shack that was provided for us as a courtesy by the real estate agent who sold our home. His name was Arnie Oakum, and if this story does nothing other than honor Mr. Oakum's memory it will have achieved a noble purpose. Mr. Oakum rescued my mother. He provided us with a roof over our heads, and he gave my mother a small salary while she trained for a job as a receptionist in his real estate office. Eventually she became his office manager.

To be fair, the house he provided wasn't a shack at all. It was small, and it was cheaply constructed, and it was badly maintained, but it was dry and warm, and when my mother got finished with it, it was clean.

For us kids, it was all a great adventure. We missed our father for his reliable habits and even his strong sense of conviction, but we didn't at all miss the times he was inflexible, and we enjoyed watching our mother in her strange new freedom. The fighting had stopped, and the house was peaceful. We found ourselves laughing freely, living the life of romance my mother believed was the sign of the good life.

Things weren't so clear for my mother, however. Sometimes she was filled with self-doubt. I can remember sitting up with her late at night as she wondered out loud whether or not she had "done right by" my father. I didn't completely understand what this meant, but I knew she was in anguish and that there wasn't anything I could do about it. She never so much as looked at another man, not once.

The low point came for my mother on Christmas of that year, 1962. There was no money for a Christmas tree. Not for any tree at all, not even a six-foot tree like the ones my father had always written into his budget.

On the first Monday of December she got out one of the hammers my father had left behind, and she went out behind the house to where there was an old pile of lumber, grown over with grass. She picked among the lumber until she found some boards with the nails still in them. She pulled these out with the hammer until she had a large handful, which she brought in her pocket back to the house.

She cleared a space on the wall in the living room, took down the large picture of Jesus, and we helped her move aside the sofa.

There, in the space on the wall, she nailed up a large triangle to serve as a two-dimensional Christmas tree.

She outlined the shape with strings of lights, big-bulbed, colored lights to form a triangle, and then a string or two of smaller, pinpoint white lights.

To the triangle she added popcorn strings, strings that even in two dimensions reminded her of the war years, when nobody had anything and everybody had to make do. One of the strings had cranberries, to remind her of her gratitude that all of her brothers had returned safe from the front.

Then she hung the ornaments. There wasn't much space, so she carefully chose which to hang and which to leave sleeping in their boxes for another year. She included one from each of her brothers and her sister, and one from each of us children. She hung pictures of our cousins—Nathan, Vickie, and Pudge. She paused a long time before she hung the ornaments from my sister and my brother, neither of whom would be with us this Christmas. At the top, just beneath the peak of the triangle, she hung a picture of my dad.

Then, on a nail eight or ten inches above the top of this two-dimensional Christmas tree she slipped the brass ring of her mother's porcelain angel.

She paused a minute. Out of the box she drew some red Christmas napkins, folded them into the shapes of poinsettias and placed them around the base of the tree, a hopeful reminder, I think, that even in a situation like that, romance is still alive in the world.

She turned to Joelie and gave the signal. Joelie flipped the switch that turned on the lights, and all at once, magically, it was Christmas.

Then my mother sat down on the edge of the sofa and cried.

It was the first time I ever saw my mother cry. Even now I don't know exactly why she cried.

Maybe she cried because she knew that we would never again have another twelve-foot Christmas tree like the ones we'd had in the past.

Maybe she cried because she missed my brother and my sister and my cousins and my dad. Whatever had transpired between them, my mother loved my father until the day she died. Would it be as hard for him this Christmas, missing her, as it was now for her, missing him?

Maybe she cried because she knew that all she would have to put under this little two-dimensional Christmas tree would be things we would have gotten anyway—underwear and socks and T-shirts.

I sat down beside her on the sofa, right there in the middle of the living room, and I put my arm around her and she rested her head on my shoulder. She turned her tiny face up to mine, my mother did, and she said that in all her life she had never felt so small.

That was when my brothers and I decided that this would never happen to our mother again.

five

The following year, late in October and then into November, we began to save our money. This was really hard to do because we were just three boys—myself, my older brother Jim, and youngest of all, Joelie. We didn't get any allowance since my mother couldn't afford it. We made our money every which way we could.

We washed the neighbor's car for fifty cents. One time. We put the fifty cents in a mason jar that we kept behind the books on the shelf above my brother's bed.

We walked old ladies to their cars at Bud Cavender's Market up the road, hoping for a nickel or a dime for a tip. That worked out pretty well until Mr. Cavender came out and chased us away with a meat cleaver. I don't think he meant to threaten us with the meat cleaver—it was just what he happened to have in his hand at the time—but it looked menacing enough there in his hand, so we never went back after that.

Mr. Flory gave us a quarter each for helping him put up the Christmas tree lot beside his peanut stand. By my father's definition, this made us pagans like Mr. Flory was, but we fell back on our mother's opinion that what mattered was that we came by the money honestly.

Most of our money came from collecting soda bottles around the empty lots near our house—Coca-Cola and Pepsi and Grape Nehi—and turning them in for their California redemption value, which at that time was three cents a bottle. Very gradually, too gradually, the little mason jar began to fill. We checked it every night. Sometimes it seemed like we were racing a clock. I had never experienced deadlines before, and this one was terrible.

On the Monday after the first weekend in December, when we got home from school, we went for the tree.

We poured the money out on my brother's bed and counted it up: $4.57 in change. Four dollars and fifty-seven cents. Not much by today's standards. It wasn't much in December of 1963, either, but it was all we had, and it was honest money, legally earned, even if some of it had come from the pagan enterprise of helping Mr. Flory set up the Christmas tree lot next to his peanut stand.

My brother Jim put the money in his jacket pocket, and we trooped down to Ollie Flory's Christmas tree lot.

We found the only tree in the lot that could be had for $4.57. It was barely three feet tall and was so thin Mr. Flory hadn't nailed one of those crosspieces on the bottom for fear the trunk would split. He told us he had saved it out for us, and we found it laying flat out on its side behind his truck.

It had uneven branches, with a dense, thick place down on the right side and almost nothing on the top half near the left. What branches it did have were clustered all on one side, which was another reason Mr. Flory hadn't made a crosspiece base for it. It would have fallen over from the imbalance in its weight.

Looking back now I realize that Mr. Flory could have given us the tree, but he was wise enough to know that that would have made it his gift, not ours. He didn't need to sell it—we needed to buy it. He did give us a poinsettia plant as a courtesy, he said, in memory of the old days. Mr. Flory wasn't a pagan; he was a romantic.

We carried the tree and the poinsettia home triumphantly, the three of us did, trading the weight between us and making a plan as we went.

Jim and I moved the head of the sofa in the living room and cleared a place against the wall. We took down the picture of Jesus. Jim tied a string to the tree and hung it on the picture nail.

Joelie went in the kitchen and popped popcorn and made popcorn strings. He found cranberries in a bag in the freezer, and some

of these he interspersed between the pop-
corns on one of the strings.

We hung a string of those big-bulbed lights,
the kind that spread a soft glow around. Most
of the lights ended up on the lower right of
the tree where the densest branches were, but
Jim put a couple of nails in the wall to help
out the thinner part in the upper left.

We added a string of the pinpoint lights,
just one string, because we were afraid of
making the tree too heavy for the nail in the
wall and because we had to save room for the
ornaments and for Joelie's popcorn strings.

The ornaments were a problem because
there were so many, but Jim said he had to
make something called an "executive decision," which was an expression I didn't fully

understand. Then he selected out of the box one store-bought ornament for each of my mother's brothers and one for her sister. For each of the kids he added one of those Sunday school ornaments with our pictures on them. There was a photograph of Joelie, ringed in Cheerios, and a paper plate angel of me, and another of Jim. He added ornaments that had been made by our cousins—Nathan, Vickie, and Pudge.

Pride of place went to the ornaments for my brother and my sister, neither of whom would be with us this Christmas. Somewhere near the top he hung a photograph of our dad.

Then the popcorn strings, one of them laced with cranberries, to remember the war years, when people had to make do or do without, and to remind my mother of her relief and delight when her brothers came home safe from the front.

Finally, the *coup de grace*—my grandmother's porcelain Christmas angel. We added a nail nine or ten inches above the peak of the tree and hung the angel by the brass ring between her shoulder blades.

We set out the poinsettia plant Mr. Flory had given us; then we went into the kitchen to wait.

It was dark when my mother got home. Winter nights came early to our part of the country. We saw the headlights of her car turn into the drive and then held our breath as the tires crunched to a halt on the gravel of the driveway outside.

She came in by the back door, into the kitchen. She hesitated there at the door as if she wasn't quite sure what was happening. I could see that she sensed there was something different in the house.

Perhaps it was Joelie's Cheshire-cat grin.

Maybe it was the tiny bits of popcorn that we had forgotten to sweep up after making the popcorn strings.

Maybe it was the fact that we were all sitting there in the dark because we had been so excited we forgot to turn on the lights.

I think it was the smell of the pine needles. Without a word she followed her senses down the hall into the living room.

Just as she stepped into the living room, Joelie slipped past her; his fingers found the switch that turned on the strings of lights, and all at once, magically, it was Christmas.

That was the second time I ever saw my mother cry.

I like to think that she cried because she realized that even though we would never see another twelve-foot Christmas tree, it didn't really matter. Everything would be all right.

Mother's gone now, and I'll never be able to ask her why she cried that night. But I can tell you why I cried. I cried because all at once I realized that both my mother and my father had been right after all. It all had to do with the meaning of gift giving.

My father had said there was nothing at all about Christmas presents that could be reduced to a business transaction. No giving in order to get, no earning this by being good enough, no obligation, no payment for services rendered. It wasn't a matter of deserving what you got, of being good enough, of merit. It wasn't that my mother did or didn't deserve this gift from us three boys. It was that the question of deserving this gift never entered our heads. We didn't give her this gift because of who she was, either. We did it because of who she was *to us*.

My mother had said that the inner freedom to do something absolutely extravagant was the closest human beings ever come to feeling what God must feel when God is being gracious toward us, that when we give an extravagant gift we somehow rise above ourselves and become a little better than we were. "A little larger on the inside," my mother had said.

My mother looked across at us three boys—all of us in tears. She stood up straight. Without a word, all four of us drew ourselves up to our full heights, and for the first time in my life I knew what it was like to be eleven-foot-four.

That's the way it happened, the Christmas of 1963, the Christmas that I learned the meaning of grace.

Back row: Big Nate, Joyce, John, Mother, Father
Center row: Small Nate, Me, Jim
Front row: Joelie, Vickie, Pudge (Jeff)